WHO,

WHAT WAS

THE GUTENBERG BIBLE?

CF4•K

DANIKA COOLEY

10 9 8 7 6 5 4 3 2 1
Copyright © Danika Cooley 2021
Paperback ISBN: 978-1-5271-0651-2
ebook ISBN: 978-1-5271-0824-0

Published by
Christian Focus Publications,
Geanies House, Fearn, Tain, Ross-shire,
IV20 1TW, Scotland, U.K.
www.christianfocus.com
email: info@christianfocus.com

Printed and bound by Bell and Bain, Glasgow

FSC MIX Paper from responsible sources FSC® C007785

Cover design by James Amour
Illustrations by Martyn Smith

TABLE OF CONTENTS

TO CHLOE AND HANNAH.
MAY YOU ALWAYS
READ AND LOVE
GOD'S WORD.

THE MOST
IMPORTANT BOOK

Just fifty years after twelve Death Ships pulled into the harbor in Sicily, and a decade after an English professor secretly translated Latin words into English, a man named after his house defied all odds and created a machine that would spread words across the world like dandelion seeds. The interesting thing about history is it is like a line of dominoes standing on end. Every event is a result of things that happened before. Once things happen, they impact what comes next—just like dominoes knocking

each other over. To really understand our story, we will go back—just a little—to the Death Ships.

Death Ships, you may ask? Yes, that is what people called the twelve boats carrying a cargo of sailors' bodies, covered in boils from the Black Plague. Frightened harbor workers sent the ships right back out to sea. It was too late. Tiny bacteria spread to the port workers, then upward through Italy, and later the rest of Europe. The plague killed one out of every three people in just five years. The city of Mainz in the German territory, inside the Holy Roman Empire, was particularly hard hit. Perhaps one out of every two people died. The plague came twice more in the years before the man named after his house was even born.

Thirty-seven years after the Death Ships arrived in Sicily, a man named John Wycliffe felt the English people should hear the Word of God in the language of their heart. So, he translated the New Testament into English— Matthew through to Revelation. Before, the Bible was in Latin, which few people understood. John preached that Scripture is our authority—our boss. We learn God's will from the Bible, not councils or popes. John died a natural death, but because he challenged the Roman Catholic Church, his bones were dug up and burned, and his ashes were dumped in a river. John's ideas about putting the Bible in the language of the people, and his preaching of the gospel, spread through Europe.

Right around the time our man named after a house was born, the priest Jan Hus began teaching theology in the city of Prague, in what was known as the territory of Bohemia. Hus had read the handwritten words of

Wycliffe, and he also preached that the Church was made of men and women chosen for salvation by God. The Bible is our authority. Popes and councils cannot declare salvation, nor can they alter Jesus' commands to believers. For his efforts, Jan was burned at the stake.

The world was upside down. Handwritten or spoken words and ideas were buzzing through the continent.

Writing ideas by hand was slow and painstaking, and often full of error. Into this chaos, our German named after a house was born. The house was one of three owned by his father.

This house sat down the street from Saint Christopher Church, just several lanes past Saint Martin's Cathedral in the city of Mainz, which the people called Golden. Had you visited, you could have

strolled past the Cathedral, the Town Hall, and the Mint where the coins were struck. You would pass a church with a three-story tower, then arrive at the house with two three-story wings shaped like an L.

Gutenberg, which was the name of the house, once bore the name Judenberg, or Jewish Hill. It was named for the family who lived there more than 150 years before. Golden Mainz was once home to the largest

Jewish community in Europe. The house, though, was seized when Jews were expelled by mourning citizens who wrongly blamed Jewish people for the Black Plague. Its name became the Gutenberg, which means the Good Mountain. Johann Gensfleisch zum Gutenberg, the name of our inventor, means John Gooseflesh of the Good Mountain. Johann was born into this sturdy structure where his invention would later change the way words are shared.

God once told the prophet Isaiah his Word would always do his will: "Rain and snow fall from the sky and don't return until they have watered the ground. Then the ground causes the plants to sprout and grow, and they produce seeds for the farmer and food for people to eat. In the same way, my words leave my mouth, and they don't come back without results. My words make the things happen that I want to happen. They succeed in doing what I send them to do."

Our man named after a house is a bit mysterious, like many people in history. All we know of Johann Gutenberg's life comes from twenty-eight legal documents, only one written in his own hand. We don't even know when Johann was born. We guess it was sometime between 1394 and 1400, give or take a few years.

We do know that our great God is in control of all history—every event and every salvation. God cares about his Word, and he sends it forward into the world to accomplish his will. The Bible carries God's Word to us, and through Scripture we are told God's great plan for our salvation. It was through Johann Gutenberg that God's Word spread like dandelion seed in the wind, bringing life to the world. This is the true tale of Johann's marvelous invention, the world's most important book, and the way it all glorified our amazing God.

WHO WROTE THE BIBLE?

There are a lot of books in the world, all of them written by people. The Bible, though, is different. The Bible was written by about forty men. There were shepherds and fishermen, a doctor, religious leaders, even kings who wrote parts of God's Word. The Bible was written over a period of 1,500 years, on three continents and in three different languages.

While the Bible has human authors, the thing that really sets it apart from every other book on earth is that it was also written by God. Scripture tells us it is "breathed out by God" and written by men "carried along by the Holy Spirit." It is both divine and human. God the Holy Spirit told the Scripture's authors what to write. They wrote the Bible with their own personality, but they told the truth about God and his instructions to us.

WORDS ACROSS
THE WORLD

Can you imagine a world without alphabets, books, or even paper? To understand how marvelous Johann's invention truly was, and how important the Gutenberg Bible would be to all people everywhere, we must take a short trip back in time to find out how writing, and then printing, came to be.

Moses wrote the first five books of the Bible to record the history of God's people for us to read, even today. Long before Moses wrote Genesis,

Exodus, Leviticus, Numbers, and Deuteronomy, people were communicating through writing. What began as symbolic pictures on rocks became alphabets and scrolls. Bookmaking may have taken off in Europe, but the inventions that allowed books to be created were really the work of people all over the world.

Our man of the Good Mountain—or Johann Gutenberg—needed three things in order to create a book. First, he needed a mixture of metals to create strong letters for stamping ink. Johann also needed paper. Last, our man needed a machine to press his metal letters onto a page. During Johann's time, in the land of Germany, metal workers and craftsmen were abundant. Johann gathered all the pieces he needed to print the most important book in the world, the Bible, and he put them together like a puzzle.

Can you imagine hauling around a book written on rocks? Or creating a library with pages made of animal skins? Reading a scroll created from dried reeds was a good idea in the deserts of Egypt, but that same scroll would rot on the damp coast of Greece. Around seventy years after the resurrection of Jesus, in 105 AD, a Chinese court official named Cai Lin mashed together old rags, fish nets and bark, and combined the mess with a strong chemical from sticky rice. He dried his mashed-up concoction on webbing, making paper. Five hundred years later, Buddhist monks took paper to Korea and Japan. Two centuries after that, Chinese people captured by Muslims brought paper to the world of Islam in the Middle East. By the 1100s, Muslim

raiders carried papermaking to Spain. Chinese painted letters onto their soft, raggy paper with brushes. But, Europeans used quill pens made from sharpened feathers or bone. Europeans needed sturdier paper. They added glue—perhaps made by boiling the bones of fish—to their paper mixture.

While paper was making its way across the world, scribes in Egypt experimented with stamping pictures on tile. China tried metal alphabet stamps made of tin, then letters made of copper. A little over 150 years before our enterprising Johann was born, the Koreans created a moveable metal type. With thousands of letters in their alphabet, printing in Asia struggled to take off. The job was just too complex. The Mongolians didn't work on creating an alphabet. Instead, they found success printing money from blocks on the bark of the mulberry tree.

In Johann's time, Europe had paper and metal alloys—strong mixed metals. There were metal artisans and metal mines. Europe had a manageable alphabet of just twenty-six English and German letters, give or take a few for other languages—Spanish has twenty-seven. What Europe and the world did not have was a method to create metal letters and a press on which to ink the letters in the correct order, then push them against the paper. That is where our enterprising Johann comes in.

By the time our creative genius appeared on the scene, universities were being established in major European cities. These centers of reading and writing were filled with students—but not with books. During Johann's youth, priests often preached without Scripture. There was a real need for Bibles people

could access and afford. Johann saw that deep need for God's Word and he met it with the most splendid of inventions, the printing press.

In the forty-five years following Johann's invention—up until the very last day of the year 1500, there was an explosion of book printing. In that short period of time, ten million books were printed—over forty thousand titles. That's a lot of books. It would have taken every scribe on the continent of Europe

over a thousand years to hand copy ten million books. That made the printing press a pretty big deal.

Gutenberg's printing press helped more people learn to read. More students and scholars were able to share their ideas and read the ideas of others. Soon, political cartoons were invented and news was widely shared. Most importantly, people were able to read, study, and preach from the Word of God—often for the first time. Johann's invention and his printed Gutenberg

 Bible were so important, historians gave the years from 1455 to 1500 a name. They call it the incunabula. In Latin, that means swaddling clothes. The German name for the infancy of printing is Wiegendruck. Even the Japanese have a name for the cradle period, calling it yoran-kibon. The printing press was world-changing—and Johann printed the most important book in the history of the world. That was the biggest deal of all.

SCRIBES IN EUROPE

"Writing is excessive drudgery. It crooks your back, it dims your sight, it twists your stomach and your sides." This scribe, copying a book by hand, could no longer contain his unhappiness. He wrote his complaint in the margin of his work. Other scribes also logged their misery on pages of books: "Oh, my hand!" and "Thank God, it will soon be dark."

Scribes were a special group of craftsmen who painstakingly copied books. Writing two careful pages a week, one book might take two months or even a year to copy. Two scribes spent five years copying a large Bible commentary. The next year, a printing press produced 500 copies of the commentary without mistakes—or written complaints—in a week.

Hand-copied books were expensive and hard to find. The biggest libraries in Europe had about 2,000 volumes, but most scholars didn't own even one book.

A RESTLESS
INVENTOR

During the Middle Ages, people were born into their position in life. In the country, there were nobles, knights, and peasants. In cities like Mainz, people

were born into their class as either patricians or as craftsmen.

Patricians were the noblemen of the cities. Johann's father, Friele, owned a farm, the Gutenberg house, and an estate in Eltville that came from Johann's mother, Else. Patricians like Friele held prestigious jobs and could serve as mayors or city councilors. Friele worked at the mint in Mainz, where coins were struck and money was handled.

Cities earned money to grow and fortify when patricians loaned them a large pile of gold coins, called gulden. The city promised to repay the money

in twenty years, then pay the patrician—and their descendants—a yearly amount called an annuity, forever. This arrangement quickly became expensive for cities. By the time Johann was in his forties or fifties, the city of Mainz was nearly bankrupt.

The craftsmen in medieval cities were practical artists who specialized in one skill. These artisans served others by creating important products to be used in daily life. Craftsmen were organized into guilds based on their specialty. There were guilds for stonemasons who built walls, tailors who sewed clothing, blacksmiths who worked with iron, and cobblers who put together shoes. In all, Mainz had thirty-four guilds. Because it was on a river, the city was a busy place with men fishing, ships delivering goods, and muddy streets lined with craftsmen hawking their products.

Johann was part of neither the patrician nor the craftsman class. You see, his patrician father had

married Else, whose father was a shopkeeper. This meant that although Johann was able to split his father's annuity with his brother and sister, he couldn't hold a job in the mint or in any prestigious position. Johann seemed to prefer the path of an inventor and businessman, two positions nearly unheard of in the Middle Ages. However, our Johann of the Good Mountain was not like most medieval young men. He set out to make his fortune based on hard work and new ideas. First, though, Johann needed a craft.

Johann became a goldsmith, learning how to make coins in a metal mold by striking them with a die created from a metal punch. This skill served him well in his future inventions. He was restless but soon devised a way to use his goldsmithing creatively. By 1428, Johann was in his late 20s or early 30s. The patricians and craftsmen of Mainz argued bitterly

over who should run the city. Patricians were draining the city bank accounts with their annuity payments while craftsmen were working hard and their income was taxed. The craftsmen kicked the patricians out of Mainz. Johann was part patrician, so he moved 150 miles up the Rhine to the city of Strasbourg where he devised a plan. Once every seven years, the people of Germany would travel to the Aachen Cathedral, under which was buried the body of the Roman Emperor Charlemagne, who died more than 600 years earlier. They would view the Cathedral's relics— bits of bone, metal, and cloth the Roman Catholic Church said belonged to saints. People hoped their pilgrimage and the viewing of relics would mean they could go to heaven. Maybe, they thought, the relics had healing powers. If one held up a mirror in the room of the relics, it might soak in the magic of the relics from all directions. This was so widely believed, around 140,000 people visited the tomb of Charlemagne in 1432 to do just that.

Now, these ideas are not in the Bible. Not at all. The people hadn't read the Bible, though, so they believed in silly, magical things like healing powers radiating from bits of bone that could be captured by mirrors.

Johann, being a businessman at heart, saw an opportunity to earn serious cash from the sale of mirrors to Aachen pilgrims in the 1439 pilgrimage. He opened a shop to make 32,000 metal badges with saints up the sides of them. In the center, he would place a polished mirror made of metal. For this grand endeavor, Johann would need 600 gulden, a shop with a press to stamp out little mirrors and badges, and a team of craftsmen. Johann found three men to finance his work, established his workshop, and began making mirrors. By a strange turn of events, the Aachen pilgrimage was delayed a year because of another plague outbreak, one of Johann's partners died, and Johann sued to end the partnership.

We don't know everything Johann was doing in Strasbourg, but we know he had begun work on a new and secret project involving a press, forms, and metal pieces. Then, our man of mystery disappeared from the pages of history for four years, leaving no clue to his whereabouts. He later returned to Mainz—to the house he was named for—with his workmen, his secret art, and a vision. Johann was going to print books.

WHY THE BIBLE?

Why did Johann Gutenberg print the Bible? Printing the Bible was hard—it took years, and a dedicated print shop. Remember, Johann is a man of mystery. We don't know how he felt.

We do know the new German Cardinal, Nicholas of Cusa, loved the Church, hated corruption, and wanted Christian unity. He thought all believers could worship God together if the Bible was available in Latin.

Johann and Nicholas of Cusa were in Mainz at the same time. Did Nicholas meet Johann, the local—and only—printer? Did he share his vision for a Latin Bible for everyone? We can only guess.

We do know that God is in charge of all events throughout history. It's not surprising that Johann printed a Bible everyone in the Holy Roman Empire could read. Remember what God told Isaiah? His Word will go out and accomplish his purpose.

JOHANN'S
MARVELOUS MACHINE

When Johann's sister Else died in 1448, he inherited the house where he was born. Johann returned to his hometown of Mainz, the city of 350 monasteries and convents. Forty spires rose high above the city walls, and the muddy streets were crowded with merchants

and citizens going about their daily tasks. Rats and pigs wandered the streets, looking for a meal. The smell was overwhelming, as people poured their toilet buckets and trash out the windows into trenches dug beside each street. Rope makers and leather workers toiled in shops or stalls along the road, adding the noise of their craft to the general din of the city. It was the perfect place for Johann to quietly perform his secret arts.

Johann talked his cousin, Arnold Gelthus, into borrowing 150 gulden for him. One could staff a house

with helpers like a cook, butler, and maid for fifteen years with that sum, but Johann had bigger plans. Johann's six employees from his shop in Strasbourg arrived to set up and run his mysterious workshop. There was Lorenz Beildeck and his wife. They swept the shop and scrubbed ink from the equipment. Hans Dünne was a punch cutter, making the letters that filled the forms of each page. Heinrich Keffer, Berthold Ruppel, and Johann Mentelin filled out Johann's team.

Gradually, our mysterious businessman added more assistants.

Every business has something called overhead. That's the money a businessperson must pay to keep the business running. Perhaps the term originated from the quest to keep a roof over the head of the workers.

Some businesses in the Middle Ages had low overhead costs. A fisherman might need only a fishing pole and a net. Printing, on the other hand, was a business with a lot of overhead cost. Johann Gutenberg had to pay the salary for employees, then purchase metal and wood to build his equipment. He gathered paper, the ingredients for ink, and vellum— the smooth skin of calves. Vellum was softer and nicer than paper, but much more expensive.

It took time for Johann to make money, so he borrowed gold coins to fund his dream of printing the Bible. In fact, he borrowed a lot of money. At first, there were small loans, but in 1449, our restless businessman borrowed 800 gulden at six percent interest from a goldsmith and merchant, Johann Fust. Today, that's around £100,000 or $150,000. How long would it take you to earn that much money from your allowance?

Now, other people's money is never free, so our Johann promised to pay the interest on the loan. That's the extra six percent Fust charged Johann when he loaned him the money. Johann agreed to pay interest every year until the 800 gulden was returned to Fust. If he did not pay, Fust could have Johann's equipment, fonts, supplies, and his projects as well. Ouch. You would think Johann would pay the interest on his loan,

wouldn't you? You would be wrong. Instead, Johann poured every cent he made into his employees, workshop, and printing.

By the time Johann Gutenberg asked Fust—the other Johann—for another loan, he owed the original 800 gulden plus 140 gulden in interest. That's the thing about interest. If you don't pay interest, it grows and keeps growing. Still, Fust wanted Johann to print

a Bible. In 1452, he loaned him another 800 gulden. Of course, Johann again promised to pay interest—a pledge he didn't keep.

It seems our man named after a house promised Fust he would work only on printing the Bible. But, there was paper to buy and ink to make, staff to pay and printing presses to build. All of that required funds. It seems Johann printed smaller jobs from the Gutenberg house that could be sold quickly to turn a profit and to practice his new art of making books. There was a short twenty-eight-page Latin textbook, the Donatus, which all students were required to use. Johann made calendars, too, and a one-page prayer to be hung in homes.

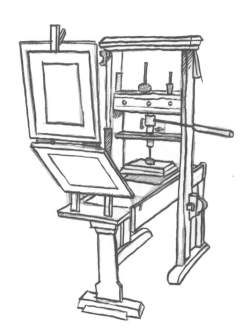

For the Roman Catholic Church, Johann printed indulgences. Indulgences were pieces of paper, signed by the pope, which promised the forgiveness of sin. Only Jesus can forgive sins, but the pope used his indulgences to raise money. The pope paid armies to attack the Ottoman Turks, a people Europeans had been warring against for centuries. Just five years after Johann returned to Golden Mainz, the Turks conquered Constantinople, the capital of the Eastern Roman Empire, changing its name to Istanbul and expanding the Ottoman Empire.

Did Johann worry about printing papers promising salvation for the Church? It is possible he was simply pragmatic. That is a big word for someone who does whatever needs to be done to reach their goal.

The Bible tells us a lot about itself. The Bible says it is sacred, active, living, and encouraging. It is the bread of life and a lamp to our feet. God's Word teaches, corrects, and trains us. It is always true, never wrong. Maybe Johann wanted to print the Bible so badly, he overlooked the Church trying to sell salvation.

THE WORK OF PRINTING

Johann Gutenberg's artisans worked together to invent the printing press and all its components, becoming experts in their field. There were several jobs at printing houses, and each craftsman specialized in his own craft.

Skilled metalworkers created the hand cast pieces of type, about four letters per minute. The metal that punchmakers poured into their handheld molds was 621 degrees Fahrenheit, or 327 degrees Celsius. Your mom bakes cookies in the oven at just 350 degrees Fahrenheit which is about 176 degrees Celsius.

A compositor placed alphabet letters into a long compositor's stick to make sentences. Once a line of type was ready, the compositor slid the line into a form, creating a page of text.

Two pressmen operated the press, inking the form and pressing the paper onto it.

Johann's two print shops eventually had a team of twenty to thirty employees working to create the world's first printed Bible.

THE GUTENBERG
BIBLE

Johann opened a second print shop in Schusterstrasse, where he printed the Bible that would one day be named for him. Just a half-hour walk from the Gutenberg press, the shop at the Hubrechthor house grew from just one press to a total of six.

First, Johann developed a beautiful font that looked like the hand-written calligraphy of scribes. He invented, too, perfectly aligned columns of type with neat edges. The letters stood like little soldiers in forty-two perfect rows. For a long time, the Gutenberg Bible was called the Forty-Two Line Bible.

Codex Berlin Folio

The Helmasperger Notarial Instrument

Johann used an oil-based ink formula invented two decades earlier by the Belgian artist Jan van Eyck. Over 500 years later, the glossy ink still stands above the page.

Next, Johann needed the best paper for 150 to 175 copies. Paper from German mills just wouldn't do, so he imported more than 200,000 handmade pages from Italy. For the 35 or 40 vellum copies, Johann needed the skin of perhaps 5,000 calves. The skin was shaved, softened in a giant pot, rubbed with ashes and chalk, and stretched to dry before it was scraped.

The Gutenberg Bible was meant to be attractive, but printing pictures was complicated. So, the purchaser of each Bible paid artists to illustrate it, usually with one artist working on the capital letters, and another adding illustrations to the margins. With different artists contracted by each of Johann's customers,

Close up of Berlin Codex

The Huntington Gutenberg Bible

some copies of the Gutenberg Bible are simple, with red or blue capital letters and few illustrations. Other copies are elaborately illustrated with vines, animals, and even Bible characters. Some copies even have expensive, shiny gold leaf on the pages.

Johann's customers were also responsible for having each 1,282-page copy of the Gutenberg Bible bound. The books were too large for one volume, so the paper copies were bound in two volumes. The pages were sewn together, then sewn into a support. Vellum copies were thicker, and bound into three books, or sometimes even four.

A copy owned by the Huntington Library, Art Museum, and Botanical Gardens in California still has its original bindings. The two vellum volumes weigh

British Library Gutenberg Bible

over fifty-three pounds—about the weight of a seven-year-old child. Each book has two wooden boards covered by leather. Many of the Bibles have metal clasps to hold the Bible closed. Metal feet keep the printed leather from touching the surface of the table.

Printing the Gutenberg Bible was a massive undertaking. After two full years, our enterprising man of mystery finished the last page of one of the most spectacular books ever to be printed. He and his team worked on printing God's Word for two years. God, indeed, sent his Word into the world to accomplish his will.

Pelplin Gutenberg Bible

A CRAFTY INVESTOR

Johann Fust pre-sold small sections of the Gutenberg Bible to monasteries and convents throughout Europe. By the middle of 1455, every Gutenberg Bible was printed and sold. With the Bibles printed and the money coming, Fust sued our entrepreneurial printer for the money he owed and all the interest.

One of Johann's employees, Peter Schöffer, was Fust's adopted son. Later, Peter married Fust's daughter Christina. It was Peter who testified against Johann Gutenberg when Fust sued him. Fust took possession of the Humbrechthor printing shop in

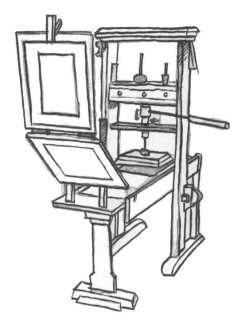

Schusterstrasse—along with the printing presses, supplies, and the Gutenberg Bible.

Johann Fust and Peter Schöffer claimed credit for the Gutenberg Bible. They also printed the beautiful Mainz Psalter in three colors with artwork, a book for the Mass, and books on Church law.

Johann Gutenberg was left with only the Gutenberg house and shop, and his small contracts to print indulgences and schoolbooks.

ROAD TO THE
REFORMATION

After the Gutenberg Bible was printed, the art of printing spread across Europe despite Johann's best efforts to keep his secret art, well, secret. In 1462, war came to Mainz. You see, the archbishop of Mainz was deposed by the pope, and another Archbishop was appointed in his place. The two churchmen gathered armies and went to war. In a twenty-four-hour period,

over four hundred Mainz citizens were killed. Eight hundred were expelled from the city, including Johann Gutenberg. He spent the rest of his life in Eltville in a small printing shop.

Sometimes the hard events in our lives are used by God for our good, and for his glory. When the printers of the

Gutenberg house left Mainz for distant cities, they set up their own print shops with the expertise they learned working for Johann. Printers began taking orders and passing on their craft to new artisans. Around eight print shops were established each year. By 1500, sixty German 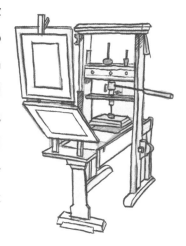 cities had printers. Some cities had at least two print shops, and Strasbourg alone had fifty. Printers worked throughout Europe—in Italy, Germany, France, Holland, Spain, Belgium, Switzerland, England, Poland, and even Bohemia.

So, what's the big deal about printing? Well, printing the Bible was a huge accomplishment. At first, it meant that institutions like universities, monasteries, and cathedrals were able to have a copy of God's Word to preach and teach from. As the process became more widespread and simpler copies were created, more people were able to own a copy of God's Word for themselves. Before Johann's amazing invention, even priests didn't know what the whole Word of God said. Now, they could read it for themselves.

Imagine living in a farming town or fishing city during the 1400s. You don't have a television, radio, or local library. There is no internet, and phones don't exist. The only news you receive is from a merchant traveling through your village, and he has his own beliefs about the news. It would be hard to share ideas with anyone outside your little town, wouldn't it? If you lived in rural Germany, you might never know what was happening in Spain—or even in Mainz. You certainly wouldn't know what the Roman Catholic Church was doing in Rome, nor would you be able to discover new advancements in science and exploration. Forget about reading a novel for entertainment.

Can you see how important printing became? Printers and the words they produced served an important role in paving the road to the Reformation. Once written arguments could easily be reproduced and distributed, ideas could spread quickly.

In the Church, those who loved Jesus and wanted to worship according to his Word became concerned about corruption and hypocrisy. They started to question ideas and teachings that were not supported by God's Word. They didn't just fret over sin in the Church, or whisper about it in dark alleys. Instead, they risked their lives and wrote about how Jesus wants us to live.

Slowly but surely, as the people of the Holy Roman Empire read, wrote, and read some more, they shared their ideas with one another. It turns out, many of their ideas pointed to the Word of God as our authority. It seems God sent his Word out, rolling on merchant carts loaded with books and pamphlets, pulled along by donkeys, printed by the marvelous machine invented by a man named after his house.

What happened to the man named after his house, you ask? Well, after Johann lost his Hubrechthor shop in Schusterstrasse to Johann Fust, and the War of 1462 pushed him out of the burning town of Mainz, and he moved to Eltville. There, he remains a mystery.

However, even the most mysterious of all mystery men leaves some clues about his life, and Johann is no different. The quaint town of Eltville was straight out of the pages of your favorite book of fables, with a white castle and little cobblestone paths winding past stucco houses decorated by big wooden beams. Right after Johann arrived in Eltville, a print shop appeared, where it stands to this day. From that print shop came a Latin dictionary for students, much like the Latin textbook Johann first printed from the Gutenberg press.

In a book once owned by the priest of Eltville, there is an inscription written that places Johann's quiet death

in 1468. Two years later, Professor Guillaume Fichet from the University of Paris wrote, "Close to Golden Mainz there was a certain Johann, named Gutenberg. He was the first to invent the art of printing with metal letters in a way that was fast, orderly, and beautiful."

Johann Gutenberg died without recognition, but he wasn't truly forgotten. His work, after all, was a seed that changed the world. The Gutenberg Bible was planted across Europe and from God's Word grew the gospel message.

The Bible tells us we are sinners, separated from God by our sin. But God made a way for our salvation through his Son, Jesus Christ, who is fully God and fully man. We need only to believe on Jesus and confess him with our mouths, and we will be saved. Jesus will give us a new heart and the Holy Spirit will live in us. God will help us repent of our sins and clean us of all unrighteousness. No paper from the Church can save us.

Slowly, that truth began to reach the hearts of people.

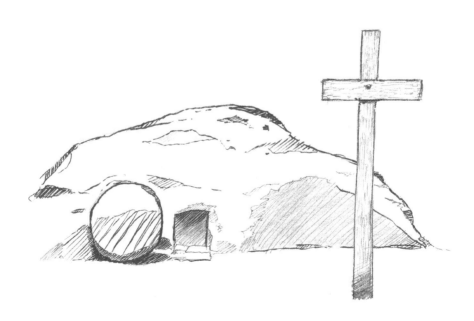

THE RENAISSANCE

During the 1400s and 1500s, the people of Italy produced amazing artwork, music, political ideas, religious writings, and scientific discoveries. We call this time period the Renaissance, when big thinkers and careful researchers gathered in Italy to read books, study the Bible, and discuss their big ideas. They came from Constantinople after it was conquered by the Turks, and from places like Mainz after the War of 1462.

Ideas matter. Scholars who studied ancient texts were called humanists—they cared deeply about human thoughts, but not about God's thoughts. Their ideas sometimes hurt people. Christian humanists, on the other hand, were interested in what other people had to say about God's Word. What God has to say will always go forth and bring about his will.

THE BIBLE IN
LATIN

You and I have been talking about the story of Johann Gutenberg and his extraordinary Forty-Two Line Bible. But the story of the Gutenberg Bible's text started much earlier. In order to understand the Bible Johann printed in Latin, you'll want to know about how the Bible came to be in this language.

The Old Testament was written in Hebrew with a few chapters in Aramaic, long before the Roman Empire existed. Many years before Jesus was born, Jewish scholars translated the Old Testament into Greek, the language of the Roman Empire. The common language helped the gospel spread widely.

They called this Greek translation the Septuagint. That's a Latin word that means seventy. Why is the first Old Testament called Seventy? There is a legend that seventy-two scholars translated the Old Testament in just seventy-two days. That's probably not true, but it's a fun way to remember a long word like Septuagint.

Three hundred years later, Latin replaced Greek as the main language people wrote and read in. So, the whole Bible was translated into Old Latin. The Old Testament was translated from the Septuagint. It was a translation of a translation, which can be a problem.

It's best to translate the Bible from the most accurate manuscripts in the original language. The Old Latin versions of the Bible were important because they allowed missionaries to share the good news of Jesus Christ throughout the Roman Empire.

61

Still, Damasus, the bishop of Rome, wanted a Latin copy of the Bible from a skilled translator. That person would have to know Greek and Hebrew—and maybe a little Aramaic, too. He dreamed of one Bible the whole Roman Empire could use.

Around the same time, a brilliant Roman named Jerome, traveling through Gaul, decided to become a Christian hermit. Hermits were like monks who lived alone in the desert. In the deserts of Syria, he spent time reading the Bible and learning Hebrew, the language of the Old Testament. He hoped this would distract him from thinking about the ungodly things he had read and seen while in Rome.

By 382, Jerome was back in Rome, working as a translator for Bishop Damasus. Jerome was the brilliant scholar Damasus had been looking for. The bishop paid Jerome to translate the New Testament from the Old Latin. Instead, Jerome used the original Hebrew and Greek to make his translation. Jerome finished his Latin translation of the Gospels in 384, and Damasus died without seeing the New Testament completed.

People didn't like Jerome's new translation of the Bible. They were used to the Old Latin. Plus, Jerome sometimes used words he thought everyone could understand instead of really hard, scholarly sounding words. The people called Jerome's translation the Vulgate because they thought it was vulgar and common. Jerome responded by saying: "If they dislike water drawn from the clear spring, let them drink of the muddy streamlet". He meant that the original languages were the inspired Word of God. Jerome believed that the Bible should be in the language of the people, which was Latin at the time, but he wanted the translation to be as close to the original languages as possible.

Jerome traveled again. In Bethlehem in Israel, he met a widow with a mansion, Marcella. Marcella

and her friend Paula both loved the Bible and were excellent scholars. Jerome lived in Marcella's mansion while she took care of his needs financially so he could translate the rest of the Bible into Latin. The task took him twenty-three years—until 405. Later, Jerome wrote commentaries on almost every book of the Bible.

Jerome's Vulgate may not have been popular when it was first made available, but it soon became the

version everyone in the Roman Empire—and then the Holy Roman Empire—wanted to read for more than a thousand years. In fact, Johann Gutenberg printed the Vulgate from his presses in 1455. Jerome would have been surprised to see that his faithful translation of God's Word was the first significant book to be printed in Western history, over a thousand years after his death.

Maybe Jerome would have been a little dismayed, too. After all, he wanted the Bible to be a translation of the original text into the language of the people. By the time of Johann Gutenberg, the people of Europe spoke many different languages. Latin, however, was the language of the Roman Catholic Church. The Vulgate was the translation the Catholic Church used—and it still is today.

In 1546 at the Council of Trent—almost 100 years after the Gutenberg Bible was printed, the Roman Catholic Church stated the Vulgate is the "approved" and "authentic" version of the Bible, and no one can reject it. That stance was a problem for Reformation leaders who felt, like Jerome, the Bible should be in the language of the reader. The Council also made it illegal to print the Word of God in any language, unless by permission of the Church. They decreed no one but the Church could interpret the Scriptures—unless that person agreed with every teaching of the Church.

Now, the idea that God's people can't read, interpret, translate, and print God's Word is a pretty big part of why the Reformation occurred. But that, my friend, is another story for another day.

JEROME'S STRANGE IDEAS

Jerome was a brilliant man with some very strange ideas. He was born around the year 345 in the little town of Stridon, Italy. That's a little over 300 years after Jesus died, then rose again. Jerome was gifted at languages, and easily learned Greek and Latin at school in Rome.

Jerome wrote about a few of his strange ideas about what the Bible taught. One funny idea no one follows today was he should never wash his body, because Jesus had permanently washed away his sins. Jerome talked Marcella and Paula into avoiding baths, too. The beautiful mansion Marcella owned must have been a little smelly!

THE LANGUAGE
OF YOUR HEART

Do you know Pig Latin? It's not a real language, but a fun way to speak in code. Let me teach you. Take a word, like church. Move the first letter, or two letters before the first vowel, to the end of the word: urch-ch. Now, add "ay" to the end of the word: urchchay. Try to read this sentence: Iay ancay eadray igpay atinlay. I can read Pig Latin. Yes, you can. It's fun, but it's hard, right? Reading real Latin is even harder.

Imagine reading the world's most important book, God's Word, in a language you don't naturally think in. You first must hear the words in another language, then your brain translates each word into your first language. Translators call your first language—the one your parents spoke when you were tiny—your heart language.

In the Middle Ages, Roman Catholic Church leaders said that only the Church could interpret the Scriptures. It was better, they thought, if common people just didn't read the Bible at all. After all, they could hear about the Bible from their priest.

Seventy years or so before the printing of the Gutenberg Bible, John Wycliffe and his followers— the Lollards, which means mumblers in Dutch and weeds in Latin, translated the Bible into English. John Wycliffe and the street-preaching Lollards said the pope, bishops, and priests weren't really the Church at all. Instead, people who were called to salvation in Jesus were the Church. John told people that if Jesus taught in the language of the people, so should we. The Church disagreed and worked hard to burn any copies of the Bible in English.

Around 1457, two years after the Gutenberg Bible was printed, two of Johann's printers—Heinrich

Eggestein and Johann Mentelin—established a print shop. They printed the first Bible in the German language. Actually, it was the first Bible printed in any heart language. The translation was horrible, but it made people think about the gift of reading God's Word in a language they could understand.

Just fifteen years after Johann Gutenberg died in 1468, a newborn baby was baptized at a little church in Germany, Saint Martin's. Little Martin Luther grew up to become a priest. Martin also believed the Word of God is our authority. We should obey the Bible over popes, councils, and priests. Martin translated the Bible into German, this time doing a good job.

At the same time Martin was translating the Bible into German and preaching straight from Scripture, an English chaplain was working on a translation of the Bible into plain English. William Tyndale spoke eight languages, but he thought everyone should read God's Word in the language of their heart. William once got into a fight with a priest who said the pope's law is better than God's law. Well, William didn't like that

idea much at all. He told the priest that if God spared his life, he would make a plow-boy—a farmer—know more about Scripture than the priest did.

William Tyndale kept his angry promise. The Roman Catholic Church would not allow William to translate the Bible, so he secretly traveled to Germany. In 1526, the New Testament was printed in English in the city of Worms, Germany—the same city where Martin was

declared an outlaw for his views on the Bible. William smuggled the English New Testament into England.

Eventually, William was betrayed and thrown into a castle dungeon for more than a year. There, he translated the Old Testament into the heart language of the English people before he was strangled and burned at the stake as a heretic. Just before he died, William asked God to open King Henry VIII's eyes. The next year, Henry approved an English Bible called the Great Bible, and put one in every church in his land. Henry didn't know that the Great Bible was really William Tyndale's translation, just under another name. Not only did William help the common farmer read the Bible in his own language, he invented many words you and I use today, like fisherman and seashore.

Today, you and I can read the Bible in the language of our hearts because of men who risked their lives—and sometimes lost them—to translate God's Word. The Bible has spread across the world because of the invention and hard work of a man named after his house who made metal letters instead of gold coins.

Do you remember what God told the prophet Isaiah about his Word? God said through Isaiah: "Rain and snow fall from the sky and don't return until they have watered the ground. Then the ground causes the plants to sprout and grow, and they produce seeds for the farmer and food for people to eat. In the same way,

my words leave my mouth, and they don't come back without results. My words make the things happen that I want to happen. They succeed in doing what I send them to do."

God's Word is powerful. It's important. It makes things happen that God wants to happen. The Bible will succeed in all God sends it to do.

THE BIBLE TODAY

One out of every five people in the world don't have access to a Bible in their heart language. Ministries like Wycliffe Bible Translators are working hard to translate into new languages. Other ministries like Open Doors USA bring Bibles to people in countries where Scripture is hard to find, and even dangerous or illegal to own.

You can pray for the workers who translate Scripture and work to distribute it. Maybe your family can work to raise money for this important ministry. Are you

good at languages, or do you like to travel? Who knows, maybe God will use you to spread his Word to others, just like he used Johann Gutenberg to print the Bible!

OXFORD

MAINZ

S

PRAGUE

-Y

THE ROMAN EMPIRE AT THE
TIME OF JESUS

BLACK SEA

MACEDONIA

ASIA MINOR

GREECE

JUDEA

MEDITERRANEAN SEA

JERUSALEM

BETHLEHEM

EGYPT

RED SEA

Capital P from the Morgan Gutenberg Bible in vellum

THE AUTHOR

Danika Cooley and her husband, Ed, are committed to leading their children to life for the glory of God. Danika has a passion for equipping parents to teach the Bible and Christian history to their kids. She is the author of *Help Your Kids Learn and Love the Bible, When Lightning Struck!: The Story of Martin Luther, Wonderfully Made: God's Story of Life from Conception to Birth*, and the *Who, What, Why* Series about the history of our faith. Danika's three-year Bible survey curriculum, *Bible Road Trip*™, is used by families around the world. Weekly, she encourages tens of thousands of parents to intentionally raise biblically literate children. Danika is a homeschool mother of four with a bachelor of arts degree from the University of Washington. Find her at ThinkingKidsBlog.org.

TIMELINE

105

Paper is invented in China by Imperial Counselor Cai Lun.

600

Buddhist monks take paper to Korea and Japan.

700s

Chinese prisoners take paper to the Middle East.

China, Japan, and Korea print books from wood and stone blocks.

1100s

Muslims take paper to Spain.

Universities become centers of writing and study in cities.

1234

Korea prints fifty volumes using moveable metal type. The system is abandoned as too complex.

1236

Marco Polo reports Mongols print paper money from blocks.

1347

The Black Death arrives in Europe aboard twelve ships. Most of the sailors are dead. Over the next five years, nearly one out of every three Europeans dies.

1384

John Wycliffe finishes the translation of the New Testament into English.

1394-1400

Johann Gensfleisch zum Gutenberg (John Gooseflesh of the Good Mountain) is born.

1398

Jan Hus begins teaching from the Bible at Prague University.

1403

The Roman Catholic Church bans many of John Wycliffe's writings.

1411-1420

The Gutenberg family is expelled from Mainz and stays in Eltville. They return to Mainz in 1420.

1415

Jan Hus is burned at the stake for criticizing Roman Catholic Church corruption and promoting Scriptural authority.

1419

Johann's father, Friele Gensfleisch zur Laden, dies.

1428/1429

Mainz artisans defeat patricians and Johann is expelled. Goes to Strasbourg.

Johann partners with Hans Riffe to make special mirrors for the Aachen pilgrimage. Andreas Dritzehn and Andreas Heilmann add funds.

The mystic, Joan of Arc, leads French armies against England during the Hundred Years' War. She is burned at the stake by pro-English troops in 1431.

1430

In January, Johann returns to Mainz after exile.

1433

Johann's mother, Else, dies. Johann inherits Strasbourg estate.

1434

Johann moves to Strasbourg.

Johann sues Niklaus von Wörrstadt, the Mainz city clerk, for 310 gulden.

1438

Plague moves from Italy to Aachen. The 1439 Aachen pilgrimage is moved from 1439 to 1440.

1441

Portuguese sailors capture and sell Western Africans, restarting the slave trade.

1442

Johann borrows funds from Parish of St. Thomas in Strasbourg at 5% interest.

1443

Johann's partnership with Hans Riffe, Andreas Dritzehn, and Andreas Heilmann ends.

1444-1448

Johann is missing from history—no one knows where he was.

1448

On October 17, Johann borrows 150 gulden, probably for the print office in Mainz.

Johann returns to Mainz and inherits the Gutenberg house when his sister, Else, dies.

Johann has cousin, Arnold Gelthus, borrow 150 gulden for him. He begins the Gutenberg print shop with about six employees from Strasbourg.

Ennelin Zur Yserin Thüre's mother Ellewibel sues Johann for not marrying her daughter.

Cardinal Nicholas of Cusa visits Mainz with Spanish Cardinal Juan de Carvajal to approve a Church worship document.

1449

Johann borrows 800 gulden from Fust at 6% interest for printing equipment, "to finish the work."

1452

Johann borrows another 800 gulden at interest. He owes 140 gulden in interest on the first loan.

1453

The Turks capture Constantinople in the Byzantine Empire and turn St. Sophia's Basilica into a mosque.

1454

Johann's shop prints a papal indulgence for Pope Pius II to fund fighting the Turks in Frankfurt.

1455

Gutenberg Bible is published in the Latin Vulgate.

Johann Fust sues Johann Gutenberg for 2,026 gulden and his print shop on November 6.

1455-1468

Johann keeps the Gutenberg house and press. He prints Donatus, three calendars, notices for the Pope, and a prayer.

1455-1500

The Incunabula, the Cradle of Printing, sees the production of more than 40,000 book titles, with over 10 million copies.

1457

Johann does not pay his interest payment on a Strasbourg debt.

Johann Fust and Peter Schöffer publish the Mainz Psalter.

Heinrich Eggestein sets up a print shop with Johann Mentelin.

1458

King Charles VII of France sends Nicholas Jenson to Mainz to learn printing. Printing is established in France. Aeneas Sylvius Piccolomini is made Pope Pius II.

1459

Fust and Peter Schöffer publish canon law, Durandus. Albrecht Pfister prints the Thirty-six-Line Bible in Bamberg.

1460

The Catholicon, a large Latin dictionary, is published.

1462

War in Mainz between the new and old Archbishop. 400 die.

Johann moves to Eltville.

1465

Johann pensioned by Adolph of Nassau, Archbishop of Mainz.

Print shop established in Cologne.

1468

An obituary notice for Johann is printed in a book years later, dated for February 3.

Print shops established in Basel and Augsburg.

1470

Print shops established in Nuremberg and Paris.

1472

Dante's Divine Comedy (1320) is printed in Italy.

1483

Martin Luther, Father of the Reformation, is born in Germany.

1493

Hartmann Schedel publishes The Nuremberg Chronicle, an illustrated world history.

1494

Girolamo Savonarola preaches against Church corruption in Florence, taking over the town. He is later burned at the stake.

1499

Political cartoons appear for the first time.

1501

1,120 print shops in 260 European towns.

The Roman Catholic Pope orders the burning of all books that do not support the teaching of the Church.

WORKS CONSULTED

Bainton, Roland H. The Reformation of the Sixteenth Century. Beacon Press, 1952, pp. 3-76.

Brown, Perry. "Preaching From the Print Shop." Christian History. Issue 34.

Brown, Perry. "Profit-Hungry Printers." Christian History. Issue 34.

The Council of Trent. "Concerning the Edition and Use of the Sacred Books: Second Decree." The Council of Trent. thecounciloftrent.com/ch4.htm. April 22, 2020.

Davies, Martin. The Gutenberg Bible. The British Library, 1996.

Dowley, Tim. Atlas of the European Reformations. Fortress Press, 2015.

Dowley, Tim, ed. The History of Christianity. Fortress Press, 2013, pp. 162-163, 287, 299-300, 305.

Duffy, Eamon. Saints and Sinners: A History of the Popes. Yale University Press, 2006, pp. 177-208.

Durant, Will. The Reformation. Simon & Schuster, 1957, pp. 293-402.

Eisentein, Elizabeth L. The Printing Press as an Agent of Change. Cambridge University Press, 1979, pp. 1-450.

Flowers, Sarah. The Reformation. Lucent Books, 1996.

Grant, George and Wilbur, Gregory. The Christian Almanac. Cumberland House, 2004.

Grun, Bernard. The Timetables of History. Simon & Schuster, 1963.

"Gutenberg Bible." British Library. bl.uk/collection-items/gutenberg-bible. April 19, 2020.

"Gutenberg Bible. The Huntington Library, Art Museum, and Botanical Gardens. huntington.org/gutenberg-bible. April 19, 2020.

"Gutenberg Bible – Pelplin Copy." Facsimile Finder. facsimilefinder.com/facsimiles/gutenberg-bible-facsimile. April 19, 2020.

"Gutenberg's Bible – The 42 Line Bible (Codex Berlin)." Ziereis Facsimiles. ziereisfacsimiles.com/gutenbergs-bible-the-42-lined-bible-codex-berlin. April 19, 2020.

History.com editors. "Black Death." History.com. history.com/topics/middle-ages/black-death. April 16, 2020.

Jones, Dr. Timothy Paul. Christian History Made Easy. Rose Publishing, 2009.

Jones, Dr. Timothy Paul. How We Got the Bible. Rose Publishing, 2015.

Lightfoot, Neil R. How We Got the Bible, 3rd Edition. Baker Books, 2010.

Man, John. The Gutenberg Revolution: How Printing Changed the Course of History. Bantam Books, 2002.

Norwich, John Julius. Absolute Monarchs: A History of the Papacy. Random House, 2011, pp. 275-298.

O'Malley, John W., SJ. A History of the Popes: From Peter to the Present. Rowman & Littlefield Publishers, Inc., 2010, pp. 171-187.

"Ornamentation." The Morgan Library & Museum. themorgan.org/collections/works/gutenberg/ornamentation. April 19, 2020.

Pettegree, Andrew. The Book in the Renaissance. Yale University Press, 2010, pp. 1-90.

Pettegree, Andrew. The Invention of News: How the World Came to Know About Itself. Yale University Press, 2014, pp. 1-116.

Popova, Maria. "Cheeky Complaints Monks Scribbled in the Margins of Manuscripts." The Atlantic. theatlantic.com/entertainment/archive/2012/03/cheeky-complaints-monks-scribbled-in-the-margins-of-manuscripts/254868/. April 15, 2020.

Rowling, Marjorie. Life in Medieval Times. Capricorn Books, 1973, pp. 113-134.

Sanders, Ruth H. German: Biography of a Language. Oxford University Press, 2010, pp. 117-156.

"Scripture Access Statistics." Wycliffe Global Alliance. wycliffe. net/resources/scripture-access-statistics/. April 23, 2020.

Thorpe, James. The Gutenberg Bible: Landmark in Learning. Huntington Library, 1999.

"Where is the Bible banned?" Open Doors USA. Opendoorsusa. org/Christian-persecution/stories/where-is-the-Bible-banned/. April 23, 2020.

Other books in the series

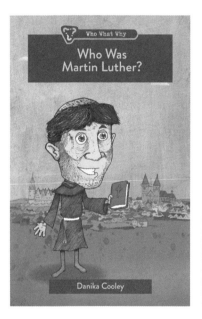

CHRISTIAN FOCUS PUBLICATIONS

Christian Christian CF4K Mentor
Focus   Heritage

CF4·K
Because you're never
too young to know Jesus

Christian Focus Publications publishes books for adults and children under its four main imprints: Christian Focus, CF4K, Mentor and Christian Heritage. Our books reflect our conviction that God's Word is reliable and Jesus is the way to know him, and live for ever with him.

Our children's publication list covers pre-school to early teens. We also publish personal and family devotional titles, biographies and inspirational stories that children will love.

From pre-school board books to teenage apologetics, we have it covered!

Christian Focus Publications Ltd,
Geanies House, Fearn, Ross-shire,
IV20 1TW, Scotland,
United Kingdom.
www.christianfocus.com